Discovering Our Place in the Universe

P9-DME-371

1543—Polish mathematician and astronomer Nicolaus Copernicus publishes his mathematical description of how Earth and the other planets all orbit the Sun, which he assumes is the center of the universe.

1605—German mathematician and astronomer Johannes Kepler determines the elliptical (oval) paths that planets follow as they orbit their stars.

1610—Italian scientist Galileo Galilei, using an improved telescope of his own design, discovers that the Milky Way is not simply a mass of dust and gas, but is instead a great number of stars too distant and faint to be visible to the naked eye.

1917—American astronomer Harlow Shapley determines that the Sun is *not* located at the center of the Milky Way.

1584—Italian philosopher Giordano Bruno declares that the stars are similar to the Sun and have planets orbiting them.

1608—German-Dutch eyeglass maker Hans Lippershey invents the telescope.

1785—German-British composer and astronomer William Herschel determines that the shape of the Milky Way is a flattened disk and that the Sun

1924—American astronomer Edwin Hubble proves that the universe is larger than our Milky Way galaxy because other galaxies also exist.

E MANLEY

JUL 10 2019

Manley, Curtis

Just right : searching for the goldilocks planet

Hudson Public Library
3 Washington Street
Hudson, MA 01749
www.hudsonpubliclibrary.com
Children's Room: 978-568-9645

To Emily, whose request for a book about exoplanets was just right   —C.M.

To Isa   —J.L.

Text copyright © 2019 by Curtis Manley
Illustrations copyright © 2019 by Jessica Lanan
Published by Roaring Brook Press
Roaring Brook Press is a division of Holtzbrinck Publishing Holdings Limited Partnership
175 Fifth Avenue, New York, NY 10010
mackids.com

All rights reserved

Library of Congress Control Number: 2018944875
ISBN: 978-1-250-15533-7

Our books may be purchased in bulk for promotional, educational, or business use. Please contact your local bookseller or the
Macmillan Corporate and Premium Sales Department at (800) 221-7945 ext. 5442 or by email at MacmillanSpecialMarkets@macmillan.com.

First edition, 2019
Printed in China by RR Donnelley Asia Printing Solutions Ltd.,
Dongguan City, Guangdong Province

1 3 5 7 9 10 8 6 4 2

CURTIS MANLEY

JUST RIGHT
SEARCHING FOR THE GOLDILOCKS PLANET

Illustrated by

JESSICA LANAN

ROARING BROOK PRESS / New York

When you look toward the stars,
do you ever wonder if anyone is looking back?

Is Earth the only planet with intelligent life?

Is it the only planet with life at all?

Our Sun is a star.

In the night sky are all kinds of stars—
more than you could ever count.
There are about three hundred billion
in just our own Milky Way galaxy.
In distant galaxies are many trillions more.

Could some of those stars also have planets circling them?

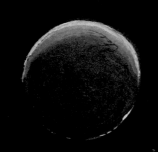

Once we knew they existed, we created a name for them:
extrasolar planets—exoplanets, for short.

Now we wonder if any of those exoplanets are *like our Earth*.
And if there *are* Earth-like exoplanets, do any of them have *life*?
And if there *is* other life, is it *like us*?

You know the story of "Goldilocks and the Three Bears":
Goldilocks finds a bowl of porridge, a chair,
and a bed that are just right for her—
not too hot and not too cold,

not too big and not too small,

not too soft and not too hard.

Our home—the planet Earth—
has everything "just right" for us.

SUN

MERCURY

VENUS

EARTH

MARS

Earth orbits in our solar system's "habitable zone,"
where a planet can have liquid water on its surface
because its distance from the Sun
keeps the planet's temperature just right:
not too hot (so all the water doesn't evaporate)
and not too cold (so all the water doesn't freeze).

HABITABLE ZO

THE MAGNETIC FIELD

EARTH'S MOLT

But liquid water isn't the only thing that matters.
Earth is just right for us for other reasons, too.

Earth is big enough that part of its core is still molten,
swirling with so much iron that it creates a magnetic field
strong enough to protect our atmosphere from the solar wind.

Earth's atmosphere is thick enough
that it keeps our oceans from drying up,
and its oxygen lets us breathe.

Without liquid water, a strong magnetic field,
and a thick atmosphere with lots of oxygen,
life on Earth would be very different—
or maybe even impossible.

But could there be life that's *different from* life on Earth?
We don't know if other kinds of life are possible
or where to look for them.

We can only look for what we do know—
life that's like the life on Earth.

So we look into the darkness, where stars like our own Sun
seem like specks of light, almost too faint to see.

Planets are much smaller than stars,
and they don't shine on their own.

For a few stars that are close to Earth,
large telescopes can actually see an exoplanet,
but only if the glare from the star is blocked—
like when you hide the Moon's glow with your hand.

But for stars much farther away, astronomers use more powerful telescopes on mountaintops or floating in space.

Kepler

Launched in 2009, *Kepler* is a telescope that orbits the Sun and continuously watches a small portion of the sky to find Earth-sized exoplanets. Part of *Kepler*'s mission is to tell us how common Earth-like exoplanets are in the universe.

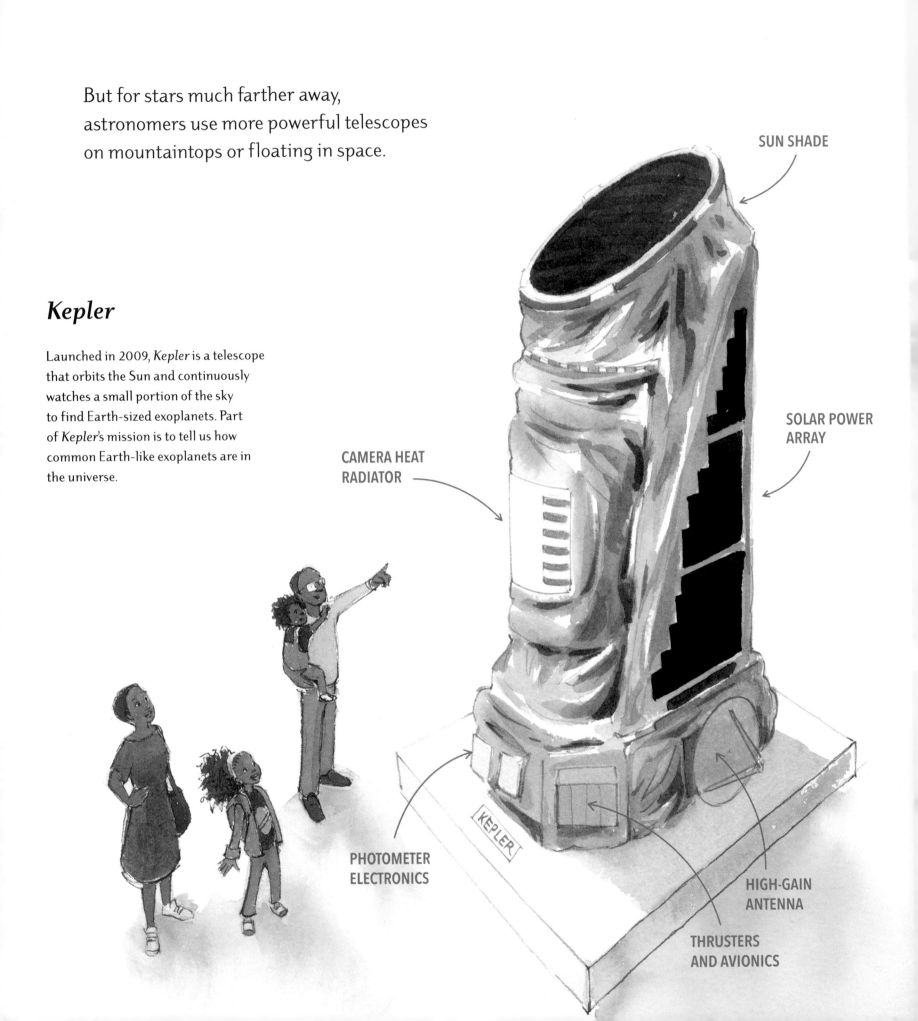

SUN SHADE

SOLAR POWER ARRAY

CAMERA HEAT RADIATOR

PHOTOMETER ELECTRONICS

HIGH-GAIN ANTENNA

THRUSTERS AND AVIONICS

KEPLER

W. M. Keck Observatory

This two-telescope observatory sits on a mountaintop
in Hawai'i and has helped scientists discover more
exoplanets than any other ground-based telescope so far.
Keck's location surrounded by the Pacific Ocean provides
excellent clarity for viewing the stars.

James Webb
Space Telescope

As big as a tennis court, the *James Webb
Space Telescope* is designed to look at infrared
light, a spectrum that is invisible to our eyes.
This space telescope will help us investigate
how solar systems form.

TESS
Transiting Exoplanet
Survey Satellite

With four cameras, *TESS* will monitor over
200,000 stars to watch for tiny changes in
brightness caused by exoplanets passing in
front of their stars, or *transiting*.

Even those powerful telescopes must use special methods for looking at starlight
to reveal the tiny clues that show some stars are not alone:

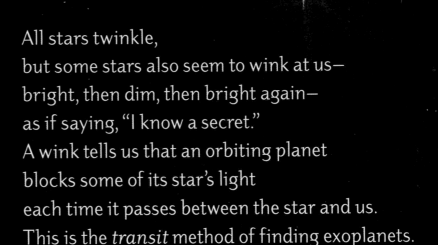

All stars twinkle,
but some stars also seem to wink at us—
bright, then dim, then bright again—
as if saying, "I know a secret."
A wink tells us that an orbiting planet
blocks some of its star's light
each time it passes between the star and us.
This is the *transit* method of finding exoplanets.

Some stars seem to wave at us—
wobbling slightly one way and then the other—
as if trying to get our attention.
Waving tells us that an orbiting planet
is tugging the star around and around with its gravity,
like a puppy on a leash running circles around you.
This is the *radial velocity* method of finding exoplanets.

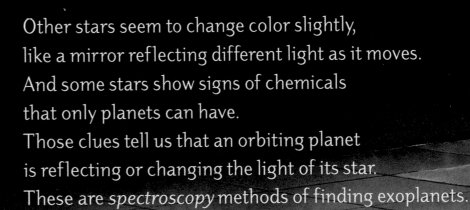

Other stars seem to change color slightly,
like a mirror reflecting different light as it moves.
And some stars show signs of chemicals
that only planets can have.
Those clues tell us that an orbiting planet
is reflecting or changing the light of its star.
These are *spectroscopy* methods of finding exoplanets.

By looking at only tiny portions of the night sky,
astronomers have found roughly four thousand exoplanets.

Based on that small sample,
we now believe that most stars in our galaxy
have at least one planet orbiting them.

When astronomers discover a new exoplanet,
they can usually figure out how large it is
by how much it affects its star's light,
and how close it is to its star
by how quickly it orbits.

Kepler-16b

Type: Gas giant
Size: 0.75 x Jupiter
Discovered: 2011
Distance: 196 light-years from Earth

This planet orbits a pair of stars instead of just one. If you could float on the cloud tops, you would see two sunsets. Kepler-16b is just inside the habitable zone, but as a gas giant, it is unlikely to be suitable for life.

If the new exoplanet is very large, it is probably a gas giant like Jupiter, so we call it a "Jupiter."

If the exoplanet is smaller than Jupiter,
but still much larger than Earth,
we call it a "Neptune."

A gas giant that orbits very close to its star
is a "hot Jupiter" or a "hot Neptune."

WASP-12b

Type: Gas giant
Size: 1.9 x Jupiter
Discovered: 2008
Distance: 1,300 light-years from Earth

This planet is very close to its Sun—so close that
it only takes just over one Earth day to go all the way
around! When a planet is this close, a star's gravity can
pull the planet into an egg shape. The star is sucking away
the planet's atmosphere and melting its surface, and it will
eventually consume the planet completely.

TRAPPIST-1

Type: Star system with seven rocky planets
Sizes of Planets: 0.5–1.5 x Earth
Discovered: 2015–2017
Distance: 39.5 light-years from Earth

The rocky planets of the TRAPPIST-1 star system all orbit
very close together. Three of the planets are within the
habitable zone of their red dwarf star.
Could there be life on these
other Earths?

Like Earth and Mars, small exoplanets
are probably rocky, so we call them "Earth-like."
If they are much bigger than Earth, but smaller than
a Neptune, we call them "super-Earths."

Astronomers have found many rocky exoplanets.
Most of them are super-Earths, but some
are only slightly larger or slightly smaller than our planet.
As we keep searching, we'll discover more.

We've already found a few
Earth-sized exoplanets
orbiting within the habitable zones
of their stars—
and astronomers estimate there may be
eleven billion more of them
just in our own galaxy.

Now scientists wonder if any of those rocky planets have water,
or an atmosphere with clouds and wind, like Earth does.
We don't know yet.
Only the stronger telescopes of the future will tell us.

As astronomers search thousands of stars for signs of planets,
they also watch for signs of life as we know it.

They watch for certain chemicals in a planet's atmosphere,
like oxygen from plants and methane from animals.
They watch for signals like those we use
for TV and radio and cell phones and GPS.
They watch for evidence of huge structures orbiting those stars.

O_2

CH_4

So far they've found no proof of life elsewhere.

So far we still seem to be alone in the universe.

But as telescopes get bigger and better,
and as we watch more and more stars,
the chances of finding life improve.

What might that life be like?

It could be simple algae floating in warm seas and filling their planet's atmosphere with oxygen.

It could be things with many legs skittering over a shallow seafloor.

It could be plants like grasses and trees, and tiny creatures leaping from branch to branch.

Maybe it's beings like ourselves,
looking up at the stars and wondering.

Or maybe it's like nothing we can even imagine.

If someday we do find evidence
of beings like ourselves,
what could we do?

Even nearby stars are so far away
that going there might be impossible.
But a radio message could reach them
in four or ten or twenty years.

Should we stay quiet and hide from them?
Or should we send a message?
And if we do send a message,
what should we say?

We could say, "Hello! We're glad we're not alone!"

We could give them solutions to useful math problems,
or recipes for making strong metals.

We could send them art and poetry and music.

Or we could tell the story of exactly how we found them:
by searching many thousands of stars for a planet
that has everything we find familiar,
a planet much like our own—
a Goldilocks planet,
a planet that's
just right.

The Science of Detecting Exoplanets

Finding planets around other stars requires high-tech telescopes in space or on mountaintops on Earth. Even the closest exoplanets are so far away and so dim that they can't be seen just by looking up at the stars. To discover them, astronomers use several different methods, each of which requires special equipment that attaches to telescopes.

When a star seems to *wink*, it means a planet is passing in front of that star, temporarily dimming the star's light. This is called a "transit" of the planet. How often the wink happens reveals the length of the planet's year (how long it takes for the planet to orbit its star one time), which an astronomer can use to determine the size of the orbit and the distance between the star and the planet.

When a star seems to *wave* or *wobble*, it is being tugged in circles by the gravity of an orbiting planet. The radial velocity method can detect that wobble by looking for changes in the star's speed and direction as its planet tugs the star closer to us and then away from us. The star's velocity can be determined by measuring shifts in the color of the star's light. A slight shift toward the blue end of the spectrum means the star is moving closer to us. A shift toward red means the star is moving away. When a star's light shifts from blue toward red and then back toward blue again on a regular schedule, that's the star wobbling, or waving at us, in response to a planet orbiting it. The way the light shifts from blue to red is similar to the way the pitch of an emergency siren is higher as the vehicle comes closer and then lower as the vehicle goes past and moves away.

When a star seems to change *color* in certain other ways, the star's light is being mixed with light reflected by one or more planets. How a planet reflects its star's light changes as the planet orbits the star. This is just like the face of Earth's Moon changing as it goes through the phases from new (dark) to full (bright) and back again. Because a planet's surface and atmosphere affect some colors of the star's light more than others, the light reflecting from the planet is different from the light from the star. Sometimes a star seems to show *chemicals* that can't exist in the high temperatures of a star itself. That tells scientists that a planet is passing between its star and us, and its atmosphere is leaving its "fingerprints" in the star's light, revealing the presence of molecules such as methane (CH_4), carbon dioxide (CO_2), and ammonia (NH_3). Detecting color shifts and chemical fingerprints depends on spectroscopy methods, which use sensitive instruments called spectrometers (a prism is a simple spectrometer) to break light into the hundreds of different colors that it's made of. Differences in the brightness of one or more of those colors can be used to figure out if the star has a planet.

Many stars are near enough to Earth that the planets orbiting them would be visible with telescopes if the stars weren't so bright. A device called a coronagraph, which gets rid of the star's glare, allows astronomers to take photos of some nearby exoplanets. One type of coronagraph, which can completely block a star's light, looks like a black sunflower.

What About Forms of Life Not Based on Carbon?

All life we know on planet Earth is based on the elements carbon, hydrogen, oxygen, and nitrogen, the first three of which (along with helium) are the most common elements in the universe. Atoms of carbon can combine with atoms of other elements to form more than one hundred million molecular compounds—at least fifty times more than the number of all other compounds without carbon.

Why do so many carbon-based compounds exist? Individual carbon atoms can easily link together in long chains, rings, and other shapes, creating very complex compounds. Atoms of silicon can also link together, as can those of sulfur and a few other elements, but only into short chains; carbon chains can link thousands of carbon atoms.

Compounds based on silicon or sulfur also lack other properties of carbon compounds that are essential for how the processes of life work—at least life as we know it here on Earth.

Selected Bibliography

Billings, Lee, *Five Billion Years of Solitude: The Search for Life Among the Stars*, New York: Current/Penguin, 2013.

Jayawardhana, Ray, *Strange New Worlds: The Search for Alien Planets and Life Beyond Our Solar System*, Princeton, NJ: Princeton University Press, 2011.

Sasselov, Dimitar, *The Life of Super-Earths: How the Hunt for Alien Worlds and Artificial Cells Will Revolutionize Life on Our Planet*, New York: Basic Books, 2012.

Seager, Sara, *Is There Life Out There? The Search for Habitable Exoplanets*, 2009, seagerexoplanets.mit.edu/ProfSeagerEbook.pdf.

Summers, Michael, and James Trefil, *Exoplanets: Diamond Worlds, Super Earths, Pulsar Planets, and the New Search for Life Beyond Our Solar System*, Washington, DC: Smithsonian Books, 2017.

Tyson, Neil deGrasse, *Space Chronicles: Facing the Ultimate Frontier*, New York: W.W. Norton, 2012.

Tyson, Neil deGrasse, Michael A. Strauss, and J. Richard Gott, *Welcome to the Universe: An Astrophysical Tour*, Princeton, NJ: Princeton University Press, 2016.

Willis, Jon, *All These Worlds Are Yours: The Scientific Search for Alien Life*, New Haven, CT: Yale University Press, 2016.

FURTHER READING

Brezina, Corona, *Newly Discovered Planets: Is There Potential for Life?* New York: Rosen, 2016.

Kenney, Karen Latchana, *Exoplanets: Worlds Beyond Our Solar System*, Minneapolis, MN: Twenty-First Century Books, 2017.

Miller, Ron, *Recentering the Universe: The Radical Theories of Copernicus, Kepler, Galileo, and Newton*, Minneapolis, MN: Twenty-First Century Books, 2014.

EXOPLANET WEBSITES

Exoplanet Exploration: **exoplanets.jpl.nasa.gov**

Habitable Exoplanets Catalog: **phl.upr.edu/projects/habitable-exoplanets-catalog**

NASA Exoplanet Archive: **exoplanetarchive.ipac.caltech.edu**

NASA's Eyes on Exoplanets: **eyes.nasa.gov/eyes-on-exoplanets.html**

TRAPPIST-1 star system: **trappist.one**

CITIZEN-SCIENCE WEBSITES

Planet Hunters: Search *Kepler* data to help discover exoplanet transits at **planethunters.org**

SETI@home: Analyze radio telescope data to help search for signals from alien civilizations at **setiathome.ssl.berkeley.edu**

AMATEUR ASTRONOMY CLUB AND STAR PARTY WEBSITES

Night Sky Network: Find a U.S. astronomy club or star party event (telescopes provided!) near you at **nightsky.jpl.nasa.gov**

International Astronomy Groups: Find astronomy clubs from all around the world at **astronomy.com/community/groups**

The Pace of Discovery

Often science moves slowly, with years or even decades between breakthroughs. But in the search for exoplanets, astronomers are making interesting discoveries every few months. During the three years it took to create this book: the count of confirmed exoplanets increased by 1,500; Earth-sized planets orbiting in their stars' habitable zones were found around the red dwarf stars Proxima Centauri (the closest star to our own solar system) and TRAPPIST-1; and exoplanet WASP-12b, assumed to look like Jupiter, was found to be darker than asphalt. An illustration or some text had to be changed as each new piece of information was reported.

1953—Harlow Shapley
recognizes the importance
of liquid water to life and
describes the "liquid water
belt" that is now known as a
star system's habitable zone.

1957—Robotic and piloted
space missions begin
exploring space, the Moon,
and the other bodies in our
solar system.

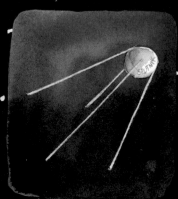

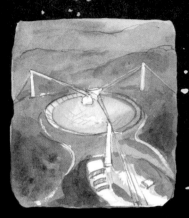

1991—Astronomers using
the Arecibo radio telescope
in Puerto Rico discover two
planets orbiting a pulsar
(a collapsed, rapidly
spinning star).

1992—Astronomers using
the *Hubble Space Telescope*
to study the Orion Nebula
make the first discovery of
disks of dust orbiting young
stars; over the next several
million years, planets may
form from the disks.

1995—American and Swiss
astronomers announce the
first definitive discovery of
a planet orbiting a Sun-like
star; this is also the first
exoplanet discovered by
the radial velocity (wobble)
method.

1999—American astronomers
using inexpensive telescopes
make the first discovery of
an exoplanet by the transit
(wink) method.

2001—Astronomers using a
telescope in Chile make the first
discovery of a planet in its star's
habitable zone; the planet is a
Jupiter, but if it has moons, they
might be habitable.

2001—Astronomers using *Hubble*
make the first measurement
of an element (sodium) in the
atmosphere of an exoplanet.